ESTONIA

Dear Saunders family!

Thank you for hosting me at such a beautiful and special place as Key West. This book gives you a little insight to a place special to my heart - Estonia, home. It's said that you should count your blessings every day. One of mine is definitely having great friends ~~like~~ like you.

Thanks again,   Ilmar.

Christmas 2008

ESTONIA

Text: Valdo Praust
Layout: Jaana Kukk
Editor: Aimur Kruuse
Photos: Toomas Tuul

ISBN 9949-411-36-X (paperback)
ISBN 9949-411-37-8 (hardcover)

Eesti. Estonia. Estland. Maalapike Põhja-Euroopas, ekvaatorist kaks korda kaugemal kui põhjapoolusest. Suviste valgete ööde ajal peitub päike vaid mõneks tunniks silmapiiri taha.

Inimene jõudis siia taanduva ürgjää kannul kümmekond tuhat aastat tagasi. Muistsete hõimude uskumusi mõjutas palju pimestava päikese sarnane taevane külaline – mõne tuhande aasta vanune Kaali meteoriidikraater Saaremaal on suursuguseim kogu maailmas.

Kaheksa sajandit tagasi toimunud ristisõjad viisid Eesti õhtumaisesse kultuuriruumi. Olulist rolli hakkasid mängima peamiselt saksa päritolu sisserändajad; Eesti kuulus tollal kordamööda nii sakslastele, taanlastele, rootslaste, poolakatele kui ka venelastele. See ajastu kinkis meile kaunid kivikirikud, linnused ja mõisad. Tallinn muutus keskajal võimsaks kaubalinnaks, meremärgina püstitatud Oleviste kiriku 159-meetrine torn oli tollal maailma kõrgeim ehitis.

Põlisrahva – eestlaste – rahvuslik ärkamine viis 1918. aastal iseseisva riigi tekkimiseni. Vahepealse Nõukogude Liidu anneksiooni järgselt taastas Eesti 1991. aastal oma iseseisvuse, jõudes napi kümne aastaga infotehnoloogias maailma tippriikide hulka. Tänane Eesti on tuntud kui edukas ja innovaatiline, äsja Euroopa Liiduga liitunud väikeriik.

Samas ei ole pooleteise miljoniline asustus hävitanud puutumatut loodust. Kõrgeid mägesid siin ei ole, kuid üle poole Eestist on kaetud metsade, soode ja rabadega, mille matkaradadel võib nautida ürgsuse ilu ning kuulata looduse hääli.

Eriti uhke võib Eesti olla oma märgalade üle, mis mujal Euroopas on tihti kuivendatud. Soomaal asuvat enam kui kaheksa meetri kõrgust Kuresoo rabarinnatist peetakse maailma suurejoonelisemaks, omapärane on ka sealkandis esinev viies – kevadine üleujutuste aastaaeg. Väga kaunid on liigendatud rannajoonega saared: kokku on neid Eestis mitu tuhat, alates suurtest kuni pisitillukesteni.

Tere tulemast Eestisse - ürgse loodusega euroopalikule maale!

Valdo Praust http://www.mois.ee/

Eesti. Estonia. Estland. A plot of land in northern Europe twice as far from the equator as from the North Pole. On bright summer nights, the sun only hides behind the horizon for a couple hours.

Man arrived here, following receding glaciers, around ten thousand years ago. The beliefs of ancient tribes were heavily influenced by a visitor resembling the dazzling sun - the Kaali meteorite crater of several thousand years ago on the island of Saaremaa is one of the most majestic in the entire world.

The crusades of eight centuries ago took Estonia to Occidental culture. Immigrants of mostly German origin started to play an important role. Estonia used to belong at different times to the Germans, Danes, Swedes, Poles and Russians. This era gave us beautiful stone churches, strongholds and manors. Tallinn became an important merchant town in the Middle Ages, and St. Olav's Church spire with its 159 meters was the tallest building in the world at that time.

The national awakening of the indigenous people - the Estonians - peaked with the emergence of an independent state

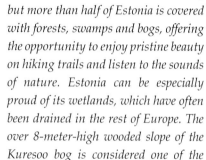

in 1918. Following the intermediate annexation by the Soviet Union, Estonia restored its independence in 1991, becoming one of the leading IT countries in the world within ten years. Estonia is known today as a successful and innovative small country that has recently acceded to the European Union.

At the same time, the 1.5 million inhabitants have not destroyed the untouched nature. There are no tall mountains, but more than half of Estonia is covered with forests, swamps and bogs, offering the opportunity to enjoy pristine beauty on hiking trails and listen to the sounds of nature. Estonia can be especially proud of its wetlands, which have often been drained in the rest of Europe. The over 8-meter-high wooded slope of the Kuresoo bog is considered one of the most magnificent in the world. The fifth season here is also unique - the spring flood season. The islands with a sinuate coastline are also very beautiful: in Estonia, there are several thousand islands, both big and tiny.

Welcome to Estonia - a European country with pristine nature!

Valdo Praust http://www.mois.ee/

Eesti. Estonia. Estland. Ein Stück Land in Nordeuropa, zweimal so weit vom Äquator wie vom Nordpol entfernt. In den hellen Sommernächten versteckt sich die Sonne nur für ein paar Stunden hinter dem Horizont.

Der Mensch gelangte nach dem Ende der Eiszeit hierher, vor etwa zehntausend Jahren. Ein himmlischer Gast, ähnlich der blendenden Sonne, beeinflusste den Glauben der Urstämme: Der einige Tausend Jahre alte Meteoritenkrater von Kaali auf der Insel Saaremaa ist der eindrucksvollste auf der ganzen Welt.

Die Kreuzzüge vor acht Jahrhunderten führten Estland in den abendländischen Kulturraum. Deutsche Einwanderer spielten dabei eine wichtige Rolle. Über Estland herrschten nacheinander die Deutschen, Dänen, Schweden, Polen sowie Russen. Dieses Zeitalter schenkte uns schöne Steinkirchen, Burgen und Gutshöfe. Tallinn entwickelte sich zu einer mächtigen Handelsstadt. Der als Seezeichen errichtete 159 Meter hohe Turm der Olaikirche war damals das höchste Bauwerk der Welt.

Das nationale Erwachen der Esten führte 1918 zur Entstehung des selbstständigen Staates. Nach der sowjetischen Okkupation stellte Estland 1991 seine Unabhängigkeit wieder her und belegt nach einem knappen Jahrzehnt einen Spitzenplatz in der Informationstechnologie. Estland ist heute bekannt als ein innovativer und erfolgreicher, kürzlich der Europäischen Union beigetretener Kleinstaat.

Die anderthalb Millionen Einwohner haben die unberührte Natur nicht zerstört. Hohe Berge gibt es hier zwar nicht, mehr als die Hälfte Estlands ist jedoch mit Wald, Sümpfen und Mooren bedeckt.

Besonders stolz kann Estland auf seine Feuchtgebiete sein, die vielerorts in Europa trocken gelegt worden sind. Die etwa acht Meter hohe Moorkante in Soomaa gilt als die höchste in der Welt. Eigenartig ist ebenfalls die dortige fünfte Jahreszeit – die Überschwemmungszeit im Frühling. Sehenswert sind Estlands mehrere Tausend Inseln, von groß bis winzig klein.

Willkommen in Estland – in einem europäischen Land mit unberührter Natur!

Valdo Praust http://www.mois.ee/

Estonia: un pequeño país nórdico dos veces más cerca del Polo Norte que del Ecuador. En las noches blancas estivales se esconde el Sol sólo por unas horas.

Con la retirada de los hielos polares, hace unos diez mil años, apareció la vida humana. Un deslumbrador visitante celeste hace varios miles de años, el meteorito de Kaali, en la isla de Saaremaa, dejó su huella en los credos de las tribus prehistóricas, siendo uno de los mayores cráteres del mundo.

La pertenencia de Estonia a la cultura occidental fue decidida hace ochocientos años con la llegada de cruzados, sobre todo de origen alemán. Poderes extranjeros han gobernado sucesivamente: alemanes, daneses, suecos, polacos y rusos. Las iglesias de piedra, las fortalezas y las residencias señoriales son la herencia de esos tiempos. Durante la época medieval Tallinn se convirtió en una importante ciudad comercial; la torre de la iglesia de San Olav, con 159 metros, usada por los barcos como referencia, fue la construcción más alta del mundo.

El despertar de la conciencia nacional llevó a los estonios a fundar en 1918 su propio estado, cuya independencia fue restaurada en 1991, tras la ocupación soviética. Estonia ha alcanzado en la última década posiciones cimeras en el uso de las tecnologías informativas, siendo considerada un miembro exitoso e innovador de la Unión Europea.

El país, con un millón y medio de habitantes, conserva un entorno virgen. No hay altos picos, pero más de la mitad del territorio está cubierto por bosques, pantanos y turberas, donde se puede disfrutar de una belleza primitiva y oír la voz de la Naturaleza.

Estonia puede estar orgullosa de conservar sus pantanos, que en el resto de Europa han sido desecados. El talud de la turbera de Kuresoo, en Soomaa, con ocho metros de altura, es uno de las más impresionantes del mundo. Una "quinta estación" se aprecia aquí: la inundación primaveral. Las islas, entre grandes y diminutas, suman millar y medio y poseen dibujos costeros de gran belleza.

¡Bienvenidos a Estonia: parte de Europa y virgen aún!

Valdo Praust http://www.mois.ee/

Эстония. Клочок земли в Северной Европе, в два раза дальше от экватора, чем от Северного полюса. В белые летние ночи солнце лишь на несколько часов прячется за горизонт.

Человек заселил здешние земли после отступления ледников около десяти тысяч лет назад. На верования древних народов оказал огромное влияние подобный ослепляющему солнцу «небесный гость» – метеоритный кратер Каали на Сааремаа является одним из самых великолепных в мире.

В результате крестовых походов, прошедших восемь веков назад, Эстония вошла в западное культурное пространство. Важную роль стали играть пришельцы немецкого происхождения; в то время Эстония принадлежала то немцам, то датчанам, то шведам, то полякам, то русским. Этот период подарил нам прекрасные церкви, крепости и мызы. Таллинн в средние века превратился в мощный торговый город, а церковь Олевисте с ее 159-метровой башней, служившей путеводным знаком для мореплавателей, была в то время самым высоким зданием в мире.

Национальное пробуждение эстонцев в 1918 году привело к возникновению независимого государства. Независимость Эстонии была восстановлена в 1991 году, и страна всего за десяток лет стала одной из ведущих в мире в области инфотехнологии. Сейчас Эстония известна как успешно развивающаяся и новаторская страна, только что вступившая в Европейский Союз.

В то же время полуторамиллионное население не погубило дивную природу. Здесь нет горных вершин, но более половины Эстонии покрыто лесами и болотами, где на походных тропах можно любоваться первобытной природой и слушать ее голоса. Особую гордость для Эстонии представляют заболоченные территории, которые в других странах Европы часто осушаются. Восьмиметровую вышку в трясине Куресоо считают одной из лучших в мире. В «краю болот» есть «пятое время года» – весенние наводнения. Весьма живописны также эстонские острова с причудливой береговой линией. Всего их несколько тысяч – есть и большие, и совсем крошечные.

Добро пожаловать в Эстонию – европейскую страну с первобытной природой!

Вальдо Прауст http://www.mois.ee/

Viro, Eesti, Estonia, Estland. Maatilkku Pohjois-Euroopassa, matkaa päiväntasaajalle kaksi kertaa enemmän kuin pohjoisnavalle. Valoisina kesäöinä aurinko painuu mailleen vain muutamaksi tunniksi.

Ihminen saapui tänne vetäytyvän mannerjään kannoilla kymmenkunta tuhatta vuotta sitten. Taivaalta pudonnut sokaisevan auringon kaltainen vieras muokkasi suuresti muinaisten asukkaiden käsitystä maailmanjärjestyksestä – meteoriitin maahansyöksystä Saarenmaalle joitakin tuhansia vuosia sitten syntynyt Kaalinjärvi on ainutlaatuinen luonnonnähtävyys.

Kahdeksansadan vuoden takaiset ristiretket veivät Viron osaksi länsimaista kulttuuripiiriä. Merkittävään asemaan kohosivat varsinkin saksalaissukuiset maahantulijat. Virossa isännöivät vuoron perään saksalaiset, tanskalaiset, ruotsalaiset, puolalaiset ja venäläiset vallanpitäjät. Maahan rakennettiin kauniita kivikirkkoja, linnoja ja kartanoita. Tallinna kehittyi keskiajalla mahtavaksi kauppakaupungiksi ja Olevisten kirkon 159 metrin korkeuteen kohonnut torni oikeutti aikoinaan maailman korkeimman rakennuksen arvonimeen.

Itsenäisen valtion synty vuonna 1918 oli seurausta virolaisten, maan alkuperäisen väestön, kansallisesta heräämisestä. Viro sai vuosikymmenten neuvostomiehityksen jälkeen itsenäisyytensä takaisin vuonna 1991 ja reilussa vuosikymmenessä maa on raivannut tiensä maailman huippujen joukkoon esimerkiksi informaatioteknologian alalla. Pieni Viro tunnetaan nykyään menestyvänä ja innovatiivisena, vastikään Euroopan unioniin liittyneenä valtiona.

Puolentoista miljoonan hengen maahan mahtuu edelleen myös runsaasti koskematonta luontoa. Korkeita vuoria Virossa

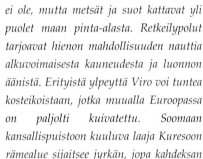

ei ole, mutta metsät ja suot kattavat yli puolet maan pinta-alasta. Retkeilypolut tarjoavat hienon mahdollisuuden nauttia alkuvoimaisesta kauneudesta ja luonnon äänistä. Erityistä ylpeyttä Viro voi tuntea kosteikoistaan, jotka muualla Euroopassa on paljolti kuivatettu. Soomaan kansallispuistoon kuuluva laaja Kuresoon rämealue sijaitsee jyrkän, jopa kahdeksan metriä korkean männikköisen rinteen laella. Omalaatuinen ilmiö on myös alueen viides vuodenaika eli keväinen tulvakausi. Saaria Virossa on useampi tuhat; joukkoon mahtuu sekä suuria että pienen pieniä, kaikki yhtä lailla kauniita rosoisine rantoineen.

Tervetuloa Viroon – eurooppalaiseen maahan, alkukantaisen luonnon helmaan!

Valdo Praust http://www.mois.ee/

Eesti. Estonia. Estland. Ett stycke land i norra Europa, dubbelt så långt från ekvatorn som från nordpolen. Under vita sommarnätter gömmer solen sig bakom horisonten endast någon timme.

Människan kom hit bakom den tillbakadragande inlandsisen för ett tiotal tusen år sedan. De forna folkstammars trosuppfattning påverkades mycket av en udda gäst från himlen som liknade den bländande solen – den några tusen år gamla Kaali meteoritkratern på Ösel är bland de mest fantastiska i hela världen.

Korstågen för åtta sekler sedan tog Estland till det västerländska kulturrummet. Invandrare av huvudsakligen tyskt påbrå började spela en viktig roll i Estland som då turvis styrdes av såväl tyskar, danskar, svenskar, polacker som ryssar. Den eran gav oss vackra stenkyrkor, borgar och herrgårdar. Tallinn blev en mäktig handelsstad på medeltiden, det 159 meter höga tornet på S:t Olaikyrkan som uppfördes som ett riktmärke för sjöfarare var då världens högsta byggnad.

Urbefolkningens – esternas – nationella uppvaknande ledde 1918 till en självständig stat. Efter en mellanperiod av sovjetisk annektion återställde 1991 Estland sin självständighet och tog på knappt tio år platsen som en av världens främsta IT-länder.

Dagens Estland är känt som en framgångsrik och innovativ småstat som nyss blev medlem i den Europeiska Unionen.

Den en och en halv miljon stora befolkningen har dock inte förstört den vilda naturen. Några höga berg finns inte här, men över halva Estland är täckt med skog, träsk och våtmark, där man på vandringsstigar kan njuta av urskogens skönhet och lyssna på naturens ljud.

Särskilt stolt kan Estland känna sig för sina sankmarker som det övriga Europa för det mesta har dränerat. Den mer än åtta meter höga Kuresoo myråsen i Soomaa anses vara bland de mest magnifika i världen, mycket speciell där är även den så kallade femte årstiden – översvämningarna på våren. Extra vackra är Estlands öar med sina ringlande kustlinjer: sammanlagt flera tusen öar, från stora till pyttesmå.

Välkomna till Estland – ett europeiskt land med urtida natur!

Valdo Praust http://www.mois.ee/

Eesti. Estonia. Estland. Une parcelle de terre au Nord de l'Europe, deux fois plus loin de l'Equateur que du Pôle Nord. Pendant les nuits blanches de l'été le soleil ne se couche que pour quelques heures derrière l'horizon.

L'homme arrivait sur ces terres il y a des dizaines de milliers d'années, à la suite du réculement de la glace. Les convictions des anciennes tribus étaient fortement influencées par un visiteur céléste au visage de l'éblouissant soleil – le cratère de Kaali à Saaremaa, datant de plusieurs milliers d'années, est l'un des plus remarquables du monde.

Il y a huit siècles, au temps de croisades, l'Estonie entra dans l'espace cultruelle occidentale. Des immigrants, surtout de l'orginie allemande, commençaient à jouer un rôle important dans le pays. L'Estonie passait à cette époque de mains des Allemandes aux Danois, puis aux Polonais et aux Russes. La période a laissé en Estonie des jolies églises en pierre, des châteaux-forts et des manoirs. Tallinn devint une ville marchande puissante, la tour de l'église de St Olaf, haute de159 mètres et servant de phare, était à l'époque le bâtiment le plus haut dans le monde.

Le réveil national du peuple autochtone – les Estoniens, aboutit en 1918 à la création d'un État souvérain . Après la période suivante de l'occupation soviétique, l'Estonie arrivait à rétablir son indépendance en 1991, et devint en moins de dix ans l'un de premiers pays du monde dans le domaine des technologies de l'informatique. L'Estonie d'aujourd'hui est connue comme un pays performant et innovant, un nouveau petit membre de l'Union européenne.

La population, atteignant 1,5 millions de personnes, n'a pas mis en danger la nature intacte du pays. On n'y trouve pas des montagnes hautes, mais plus de la moitié du territoire est couvert de forêts, de marais et de marécages, qui offrent des belles promenades et des vues magnifiques ainsi que la possibilité d'écouter les voix de la nature.

L'Estonie peut être particulièrement fière de ses marécages, qui dans le reste de l'Europe ont souvent été drainées. Les marécages de Kuresoo, sont parmi les plus spéctaculaires du monde. L'endroit est également connu pour la saison particulière des inondations printanières. Les îles aux côtes de l'Estonie forment un littoral pittorésque. Leur nombre dépasse plusieurs milliers allant des tout petits îlots jusqu'aux grandes îles.

Bienvenu en Estonie, pays européen qui a su préserver sa nature intacte!

Valdo Praust http://www.mois.ee/

Estonia. Un piccolo pezzo di terra nell'Europa settentrionale, la cui distanza dall'equatore è doppia rispetto alla distanza dal circolo polare. Durante le luminose notti estive il sole si nasconde dietro l'orizzonte solo per qualche ora.

L'uomo arrivò in Estonia dopo lo scioglimento dei ghiacci, all'incirca diecimila anni fa. Un corpo celeste che assomigliava ad un sole accecante – il cratere del meteorite di Kaali, caduto qualche migliaio di anni fa sull'isola di Saaremaa, è uno dei più noti al mondo – ha influenzato le credenze delle tribù primitive.

Le crociate di otto secoli anni fa portarono l'Estonia nella sfera culturale occidentale. Furono principalmente gli immigranti tedeschi a svolgere un ruolo importante; l'Estonia appartenne successivamente a tedeschi, danesi, svedesi, polacchi e russi. Quell'epoca ci ha regalato splendide chiese di pietra, rocche e palazzi nobiliari dei borghi. Tallinn diventò una potente città commerciale.

Il risveglio patriottico degli estoni portò nel 1918 alla nascita di uno stato indipendente. Dopo l'occupazione sovietica, l'Estonia riebbe la sua libertà nel 1991, e divenne in appena dieci

anni uno tra gli stati con maggiori competenze nelle tecnologie dell'informazione. L'Estonia, che è appena entrata nell'Unione Europea, è nota come un piccolo paese innovativo e di successo.

Nello stesso tempo la popolazione ha provveduto a mantenere la natura intatta. Non ci sono montagne, tuttavia più della metà dell'Estonia è coperta da boschi, acquitrini e paludi, dove - su appositi percorsi - si può godere della bellezza la natura.

L'Estonia può essere particolarmente fiera delle sue zone paludose che in altre parti dell'Europa sono invece state bonificate. Il giacimento di torba di Kuresoo a Soomaa (profondo più di otto metri) viene considerato come uno dei più spettacolari del mondo; particolare è anche la stagione delle inondazioni primaverili. Stupende sono le isole con le loro coste frastagliate. In totale ci sono un paio di migliaia di isole, dalle più grandi a quelle minuscole.

Benvenuti in Estonia!

Valdo Praust http://www.mois.ee/

Eesti. Estonia. Estland. Et land i Nord-Europa, dobbelt så langt fra Ekvator som fra Nordpolen. På lyse sommernetter synker sola under horisonten i bare noen få timer.

Menneskene kom hit etter at isen trakk seg tilbake for omtrent ti tusen år siden. Troen til oldtidens stammer var preget av et besøk fra himmelen som lignet på en blendende sol – det to-tre tusen år gamle Kaali meteorittkrateret er et av de mest verdsatte i verden.

For åtte hundre år siden ble Estland brakt inn i det vestlige kulturrommet i forbindelse med korstogene. Inntrengere av hovedsakelig tysk opprinnelse begynte å spille en viktig rolle. Estland tilhørte etter tur tyskere, danskere, svensker, polakker og russere. Denne perioden gav oss vakre steinkirker, borger og herregårder. Tallinn ble en mektig middelaldersk handelsby. Olavskirken ble reist som et sjømerke, og med sitt 159 meter høye tårn var kirken den høyeste bygningen i datidens verden.

Den nasjonale oppvåkningen hos urbefolkningen - estere - førte i 1918 til grunnleggingen av en selvstendig stat. Etter Sovjetunionens anneksjon gjenreiste Estland sin selvstendighet i 1991, og innen ti år nådde Estland opp blant ledende IT stater. Dagens Estland er kjent som en suksessrik og innovativ småstat som nylig er blitt EU- medlem.

Samtidig har befolkningen på en og en halv million ikke ødelagt sin uberørte natur. Her finnes det ikke høye fjell, men over halve Estland er dekket med skog, sumpmark og myr – som med sine turstier er fri for alle til å nyte urtidens skjønnhet og høre naturens stemmer. Estland har flere tusen store og små øyer. De er svært skjønne med sine buktende kystlinjer.

Estland kan være særlig stolt over sine vel bevarte våtlandsområder, som på andre steder i Europa ofte er blitt drenert bort. I Soomaa finnes den over åtte meter høye Kuresoo myrskråning, ansett som en severdighet på verdensbasis. Spesiell i Soomaa er også den vårlige oversvømmelsen, kalt den femte årstid.

Velkommen til Estland – et europeisk land med urnatur!

Valdo Praust http://www.mois.ee/

エースティ。エストニア。エストランド。北欧の小さな国。赤道からエストニアへの距離は北極からエストニアまでの距離の2倍である。夏の白夜のときには、数時間しか日が沈まない。

氷河が後退し、人々がこの地にやって来たのは約1万年前のことである。眩しい太陽のような天からの来訪者が古代の部族の信仰に大きく影響してきた。数千年前に隕石落下によって出来たサーレマー島のカーリ隕石クレーターは、世界中で最も雄大である。

8世紀前に起こった十字軍の戦いにより、エストニアは西洋文化圏となった。ドイツ系の移住者たちばかりが重要な役割を果たしていて、エストニアは次々とドイツ人、デンマーク人、スウェーデン人、ポーランド

人、そしてロシア人の支配下におかれた。他国に統治されていた時代に、美しい石造の教会、要塞、荘園が完成された。中世タリンは大商業都市となり、航海の目印として建設されたオレヴィステ教会の159メートルの塔は当時は世界で最も高い建築物であった。

エストニアの先住民であるエストニア人の民族覚醒は1918年に国家を独立へと導いていった。ソ連邦による併合を経て、エストニアは1991年に再び独立し、たった10年間でIT分野では世界でもトップレベルの国となった。今日のエストニアは成功した国、革新的な国として知られ、欧州連合に加盟したばかりの小国である。

また、人口がわずか150万人くらいなので、自然は破壊されずそのままの状態で保護されている。エストニアに高い山は存在しないが、国土の半分以上が森や沼地、湿原で占められており、キャンプ道では原始的な美しさが楽しめ、自然の声を聞くことができる。

特に誇るべきことは、他のヨーロッパの国々の干拓された土地に比べ、エストニアでは湿地が残されていることである。ソーマーにある8メートル以上もの高さの盛り上がりからなるクレソー湿原は、世界でも例を見ないところである。その地域を代表する5番目の季節と言われている、春の洪水の季節も独特である。また、エストニアには大小合わせて合計数千もの島があり、美しい海岸線を持つ島々は特徴的である。

原生自然がいっぱいのヨーロッパの国、エストニアへようこそ！

ヴァルド・プラウスト http://www.mois.ee/
（Valdo Praust）

Pealinn – tuhandeaastane Tallinn
A-thousand-years-old capital – Tallinn ◆ *Die Hauptstadt Tallinn – tausendjährige Stadt*
Tallinn: una capital casi milenaria ◆ *Столица – тысячелетний Таллинн*
Tuhatvuotias Tallinna, Viron pääkaupunki ◆ *Huvudstaden – tusenåriga Tallinn*
La capitale - Tallinn, une ville millénaire ◆ *Tallinn, la capitale – fondata mille anni fa*
Hovedstad – tusen år gamle Tallinn ◆ 1000年の歴史をもつ首都タリン

Kadrioru loss ja valitsushoone – Stenbocki maja
The Kadriorg Palace and government building – Stenbock House ◆ *Das Schloss Katharinental und das Regierungsgebäude – das Stenbocksche Haus*
Palacio de Kadriorg y la Residencia de los Stenbock, sede del gobierno ◆ *Замок Кадриорг и здание правительства – дом Стенбока*
Kadriorgin palatsi ja Viron hallituksen rakennus eli Stenbockin talo ◆ *Slottet Kadriorg och regeringsbyggnaden – Stenbocks hus*
Le château de Kadriorg et le bâtiment du Gouvernement - la maison Stenbock ◆ *Il palazzo di Kadriorg e il palazzo del governo - la casa di Stenbock*
Kadriorg slott og regjeringets hus – Stenbock's hus ◆ カドリオルグ宮殿と政府の建物　ステンボック・ハウス

Raekoja plats ja Viru tänav
Town Hall Square and Viru Street ◆ *Der Rathausplatz und die Lehmpforte*
Plaza del Ayuntamiento y calle Viru ◆ *Ратушная площадь и улица Виру*
Raatihuoneentori ja Viru-katu ◆ *Rådhustorget och Viru gatan*
La place de l'Hôtel de ville et la porte Viru ◆ *Il palazzo del Municipio e via Viru*
Rådhusplassen og Viru gaten ◆ 旧市庁舎広場とヴィル通り

Maaliline keskaegne Tallinna vanalinn
The picturesque medieval Old Town of Tallinn ✦ *Malerische mittelalterliche Altstadt von Tallinn*
La pintoresca ciudad medieval de Tallinn ✦ *Живописный средневековый таллиннский старый город*
Silmiä hivelevä Tallinnan keskiaikainen vanhakaupunki ✦ *Den pittoreska medeltida gamla staden i Tallinn*
La pittoresque vieille ville médiévale de Tallinn ✦ *Lo splendido centro storico medievale di Tallinn*
Den maleriske gamlebyen i Tallinn er fra middelalderen ✦ 美しい中世タリンの町並み

Vaateid Tallinna kirikutele
Views of Tallinn churches ♦ *Blicke auf die Kirchen von Tallinn*
Vistas de las iglesias de Tallinn ♦ *Виды на таллиннские церкви*
Tallinnan kirkkoja ♦ *Utsikter över Tallinns kyrkor*
Vues des églises de Tallinn ♦ *Vedute sulle chiese di Tallinn*
Utsikter mot kirker i Tallinn ♦ タリンの教会を望む

Öine Tallinn
Tallinn by night ◆ *Tallinn in der Nacht*
Tallinn nocturno ◆ *Ночной Таллинн*
Öinen Tallinna ◆ *Tallinn på natten*
Tallinn, la nuit ◆ *Tallinn notturna*
Tallinn om natten ◆ タリンの夜景

Loojuva päikese värvid Piiral
The colours of sunset at Pirita ◆ *Farben des Sonnenunterganges in Pirita*
Despliegue de colores al atardecer en Pirita ◆ *Краски заходящего солнца на Пирита*
Laskevan auringon värejä Piiralla ◆ *Solnedgångens färger på Pirita*
Les couleurs du soleil couchant à Pirita ◆ *I colori del tramonto a Pirita*
Fargerik solnedgang ved Pirita ◆ ピリタの夕日

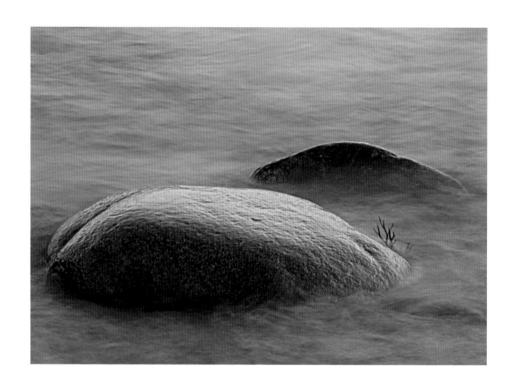

Paekallas Põhja-Eesti rannikul
A limestone coastline in North Estonia ✦ *Kalksteinufer an der Küste Nordestlands*
Acantilados calizos en el litoral norte de Estonia ✦ *Известняковый берег на северо-эстонском побережье*
Kalkkikivitörmä Pohjois-Viron rannikolla ✦ *Kalkstenskusten i Norra Estland*
La côte calcaire de l'Estonie du Nord ✦ *Scogliere calcaree sulla costa settentrionale*
Kalksteinsklipper på nordkysten av Estland ✦ 北部エストニアの石灰岩の海岸

Ajaloohõnguline Eestimaa
Estonia has an air of history ◆ *Historisches Estland*
Estonia y su aliento histórico ◆ *Дух истории*
Historia on Virossa aina läsnä ◆ *Estland med sin historiska prägel*
L'Estonie historique ◆ *Reminiscenze del passato*
Historiske sus over Estland ◆ 歴史いっぱいのエストニア

Keskajal püstitatud linnused
Strongholds erected in the Middle Ages ◆ *Die im Mittelalter errichteten Burgen*
Fortalezas de la época medieval ◆ *Средневековые крепости*
Keskiaikaisia linnoja ◆ *Borgar från medeltiden*
Citadelles datant du Moyen âge ◆ *Roccaforti costruite nel medioevo*
Festninger reist i middelalderen ◆ いまなお残る中世の要塞

Vene õigeusu jäljed – Kuremäe klooster
Traces of the Russian Orthodox faith – Kuremäe Convent ✦ *Spuren der russischen Orthodoxie – das Kloster in Kuremäe*
Huellas del culto ortodoxo ruso: el convento de Kuremäe ✦ *Островок российского православия – Пюхтицкий монастырь*
Pühtitsan ortodoksinen nunnaluostari Kuremäellä ✦ *Spår efter den rysk-ortodoxa tron – Kuremäes kloster*
Traces de la religion orthodoxe russe - le couvent de Kuremäe ✦ *Le tracce dell'ortodossia russa – il convento di Kuremäe*
Russisk ortodokse spor – Kuremäe klosteret ✦ ロシア正教の面影残るクレマエ修道院

Rahvapidu Lõuna-Eestis Setumaal…
People partying in Setumaa, South Estonia... • *Volksfest in Südestland in Setomaa...*
Fiestas populares: del pueblo Seto en el sur de Estonia… • *Народный праздник в Южной Эстонии в Сетумаа…*
Kansanjuhla Setumaalla Etelä-Virossa… • *Folkfest i Setomaa, södra Estland …*
Fête populaire au sud de l'Estonie - à Setumaa … • *Festeggiamenti a Setumaa, nell'Estonia meridionale...*
Folkefest i Sør-Estland, i Setuland … • 南部エストニアのセトゥマーの祭り

…ja Põhja-Eestis Palmse mõisas
… and in Palmse Manor in North Estonia ✦ *… und in Nordestland im Herrenhaus Palmse*
… y en la hacienda de Palmse en el norte del país ✦ *…и в Северной Эстонии в поместье Палмсе*
…ja Palmsen kartanossa Pohjois-Virossa ✦ *…och på Palmse herrgård i norra Estland*
… et au nord de l'Estonie - dans le manoir de Palmse ✦ *…e nel borgo di Palmse, nell'Estonia settentrionale*
…og ved Palmse herregården i Nord-Estland ✦ 北部エストニアのパルムセ荘園の祭り

Lõuna-Eesti puutumatu loodus
The intact nature of South Estonia • Unberührte Natur in Südestland
La naturaleza virgen del sur de Estonia • Девственная природа Южной Эстонии
Etelä-Viron koskematonta luontoa • Södra Estlands orörda natur
La nature intacte du sud de l'Estonie • La natura intatta dell'Estonia meridionale
Urørt natur i Sør-Estland • 南部エストニアの触れられていない自然

Eestis on arvukas metslooma- ja linnupere
Estonia is rich in wild animals and birds ◆ *In Estland gibt es zahlreiche Waldtiere und Vögel*
En Estonia hay numerosos animales salvajes y aves ◆ *В Эстонии много диких животных и птиц*
Metsäneläimet ja sadat lintulajit viihtyvät Viron luonnossa ◆ *I Estlands finns det en talrik skara av vilda djur och fåglar*
La nombreuse famille d'animaux et d'oiseaux en Estonie ◆ *In Estonia ci sono numerosi uccelli e animali selvatici*
Estland har et rikt dyre- og fugleliv ◆ 野生動物と野鳥の多いエストニア

Matsalu linnuriik on tuntud üle maailma
Matsalu is known to bird lovers all over the world ◆ *Das Vogelschutzgebiet Matsalu ist weltweit bekannt*
La reserva natural de Matsalu, lugar de anide de aves mundialmente reconocido ◆ *«Птичье царство» Матсалу знают в разных странах мира*
Matsalun luonnonsuojelualue tunnetaan linnuistaan ympäri maailmaa ◆ *Matsalus fågelvärld är känd över hela världen*
Le règne d'oiseaux de Matsalu est connu dans le monde entier ◆ *L'avifauna di Matsalu è conosciuta in tutto il mondo*
Matsalu fuglevernområde er kjent over hele verden ◆ 世界的な名をもつマッツァル「鳥の王国」

Suurim saar – Saaremaa – oma võludega
The charms of the largest island, Saaremaa   ◆   *Die größte Insel – Saaremaa – mit ihren Reizen*
Saaremaa, la mayor de las islas, con sus encantos   ◆   *Крупнейший остров – Сааремаа – со своими прелестями*
Näkymiä Saarenmaalta, Viron suurimmalta saarelta   ◆   *Estlands största ö – Saaremaa – med sina tjusningar*
Les merveilles de la plus grande île - Saaremaa   ◆   *Saaremaa – l'isola più grande con le sue meraviglie*
Største øy – sjarmerende Saaremaa   ◆   独自の魅力を持つ最大の島、サーレマー島

Eesti idapiiriks on Peipsi järv
Estonia borders on Lake Peipsi in the East ◆ *Der Peippusse bildet die Ostgrenze Estlands*
El lago Peipus es la frontera oriental de Estonia ◆ *Восточная граница Эстонии – Чудское озеро*
Suuri osa Viron itärajasta kulkee Peipsijärvessä ◆ *Estlands östra gräns utgörs av sjön Peipsi*
Le lac Peipus est la frontière orientale de l'Estonie ◆ *Il lago Peipsi – confine orientale dell'Estonia*
Estlands østgrense – Peipsi sjøen ◆ エストニア東端となるペイプシ湖

Lõuna-Eesti argipäev
An ordinary day in South Estonia ◆ *Alltag in Südestland*
Un día cotidiano en el sur de Estonia ◆ *Будни Южной Эстонии*
Arkielämää Etelä-Virossa ◆ *Vardagen i södra Estland*
Le quotidien de l'Estonie du Sud ◆ *Un giorno feriale nell'Estonia meridionale*
Hverdag i Sør-Estland ◆ 南部エストニアの日常生活

Tartu on 1632. aastast ülikoolilinn

Tartu has been a university town since 1632   ♦   *Tartu ist seit 1632 die Universitätsstadt*

Desde 1632 Tartu ha sido una ciudad universitaria   ♦   *Тарту – университетский город с 1632 года*

Tartto on ollut yliopistokaupunki vuodesta 1632   ♦   *Tartu är universitetsstad sedan 1632*

Tartu est une ville universitaire dès 1632   ♦   *Tartu – città universitaria dal 1632*

Tartu har vært en universitetsby siden 1632   ♦   1632年に学園都市となったタルトゥ

Värvikirev sügis
Colourful autumn ◆ *Farbenreicher Herbst*
Otoño multicolor ◆ *Золотая осень*
Syksyistä väriloistoa ◆ *Den färgglada hösten*
Les couleurs d'automne ◆ *Autunno a colori*
Fargerik høst ◆ 色鮮やかなエストニアの秋

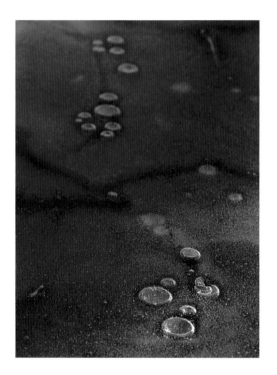

Talv katab Eesti paksu lumevaibaga
Winter covers Estonia with a thick carpet of snow ◆ *Im Winter bekommt Estland eine dicke Schneedecke*
En invierno Estonia es cubierta por un tupido manto de nieve ◆ *Зимой в Эстонии лежит толстый снеговой покров*
Talvisin Viro peittyy paksuun lumikerrokseen ◆ *Vintern lägger ett tjockt snötäcke över hela Estland*
L'Estonie, couverte de neige en hiver ◆ *L'inverno copre il paese con una cortina di neve*
Vinteren dekker Estland med en tykk snødyne ◆ 厚い雪のカーペットに覆われた冬のエストニア

Talverõõmud lausa kutsuvad nautima
You can't help enjoying the winter ◆ *Die Freuden des Winters locken an*
Los placeres del invierno nos convidan ◆ *Манящие радости зимы*
Talven riemuja on vaikea vastustaa ◆ *Vinterglädjen rent av ropar efter att njutas*
Les joies d'hiver vous attendent ◆ *Invitanti giochi invernali*
Fristende vintergleder ◆ 冬を楽しむ

Jõulukuuse traditsioon võib pärineda Tallinnast
The Christmas tree tradition may originate from Tallinn   ◆   *Weihnachtsbaumtradition kann aus Tallinn stammen*
Quizás la tradición del árbol de navidad sea oriunda de Tallinn   ◆   *Традиция рождественских елок, возможно, пошла из Таллинна*
Joulukuusiperinne saattaa olla lähtöisin Tallinnasta   ◆   *Julgranstraditionen kan komma från Tallinn*
La tradition du sapin de Noël peut être originaire de l'Estonie   ◆   *La tradizione dell'albero di natale potrebbe aver avuto origine a Tallinn*
Juletre-tradisjonen kan ha begynt i Tallinn   ◆   クリスマス・ツリーの伝統はタリンで始まったといわれている